Words on Birds

Feathered Friends of the Dandenongs

Kathie M. Thomas

ISBN 978-0-9757285-1-2
Author: Kathie M. Thomas
Photography: Kathie M. Thomas
Printer: Ingram Spark

This book is dedicated to my grandchildren and is about a collection of birds found in the Dandenong Ranges. It is not complete but covers most birds seen here.

We are, indeed, very blessed to have so many different birds in our beautiful region. The planting of native trees, bushes and plants help to encourage these birds into our gardens.

I find it a real pleasure to photograph the birds I see on a daily basis and love to share these images with my family and friends. I love it when my grandchildren ask me about a bird they've seen or heard and thought that in producing this book for them, it could also be made available for many others too.

For: Oliver, Morgan, Claudia, Katara, Josiah, Michael, Dana and Benaiah who remain my inspiration and joy for sharing the love of nature that surrounds us.

Kathie M. Thomas

Australasian Darterbird

This bird is sometimes known as the Snake Bird. This is because it has a very long neck and it dives into the water leaving just its head and neck above the water, looking a bit like a snake. This bird eats fish from lakes. The male is all black with a white stripe down its head and the female is white underneath its body.

AUSTRALIAN DARTERBIRD

Australasian Grebe

This is a small water bird and often is seen alone or just with its chicks. They build floating nests made from plants and sticks.

AUSTRALASIAN GREBE

Azure Kingfisher

This kingfisher is such a pretty bird with a very bright blue colour on its back and orange underneath. It likes to move its head up and down while watching for food in rivers and creeks and makes a tiny little peep sound.

AZURE KINGFISHER

Bassian Thrush

This bird likes to hide among the bushes and grasses. Like other birds, they like to eat worms. They are brown and cream and have a lovely pattern on their bodies.

We once had one of these birds crash into our window. It was being chased by a Currawong. I went outside and picked it up, as it was stunned, and then put it in a bush. It recovered and flew off but then visited our garden every day for months.

Bassian Thrush

Black Pacific Duck

These are very common birds in our area. They live in lakes, rivers, on dams and ponds and eat water plants and insects. They can be seen with their tails sticking up from the water, as they dive upside down to forage for food. They will sometimes seek food on land where it is very damp.

When you watch them move their wings you will see a flash of green – it looks really beautiful, don't you think?

Black Pacific
Duck

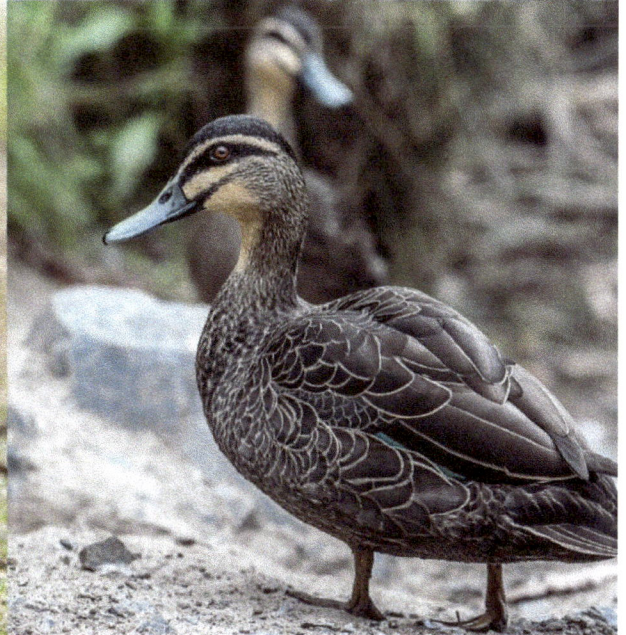

Brown Thornbill

The brown thornbill is a very tiny bird with stripes on its chest. Small birds like this one are usually insect eaters but will sometimes eat seeds and fruit. They can usually be heard in trees but not always seen. The thornbills regularly hang around together in groups.

Brown Thornbill

Buff-banded Rail

This bird has different stripes and is a bigger bird with long thin legs and three toes on each foot. They are often alone or sometimes with one other Rail, and they like to hang around wetlands and lakes.

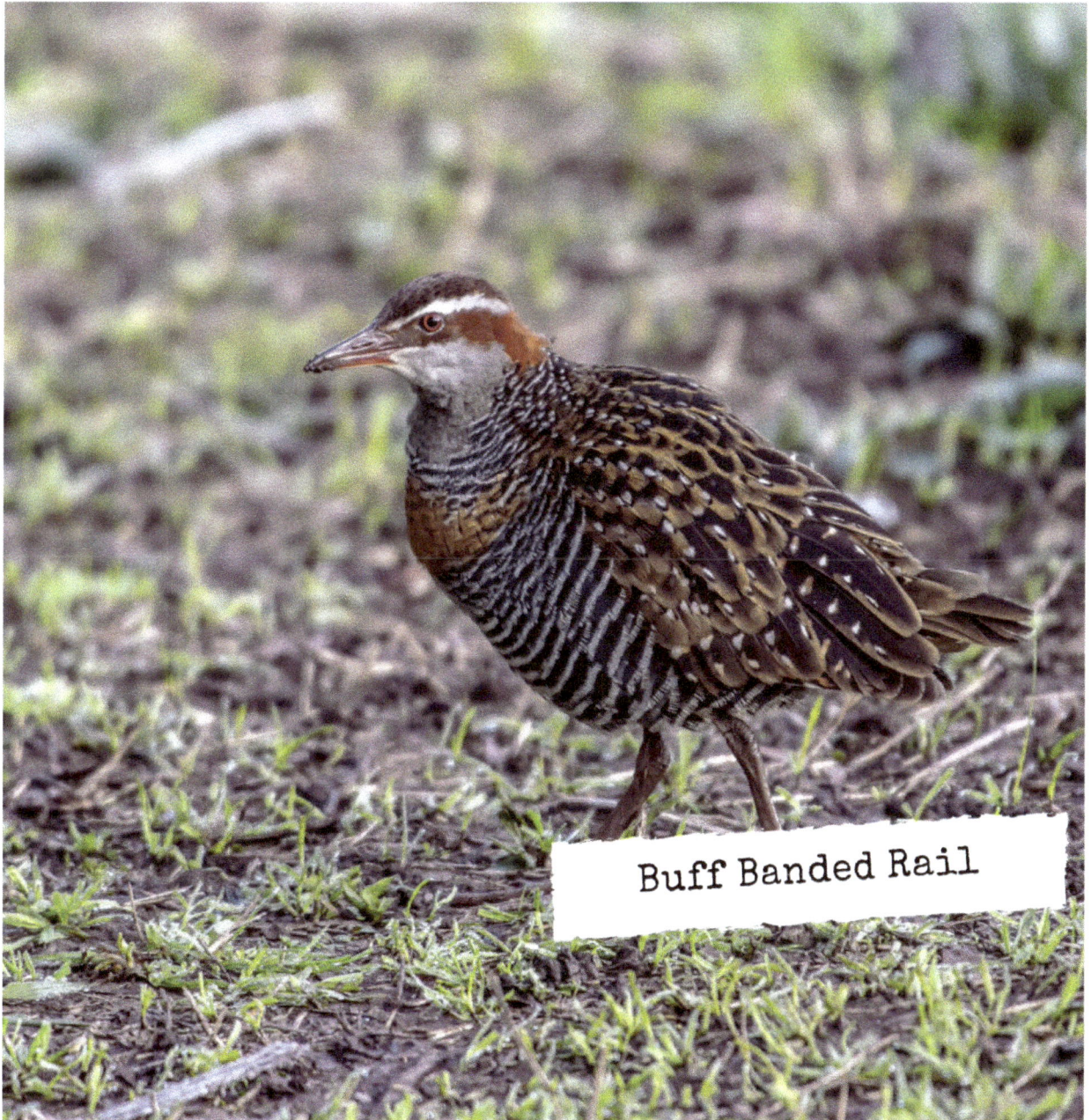

Buff Banded Rail

Crimson Rosella

Crimson Rosellas have red bodies and blue wings. But their babies and young ones are green before maturing into adult colours. They often hang around in groups and can be quite noisy. They like to eat seeds of bushes and grasses as well as insects, and they like fruit too. So, if your parents have fruit trees, they might have to cover the fruit when it's growing so the birds don't eat them all.

CRIMSON ROSELLA

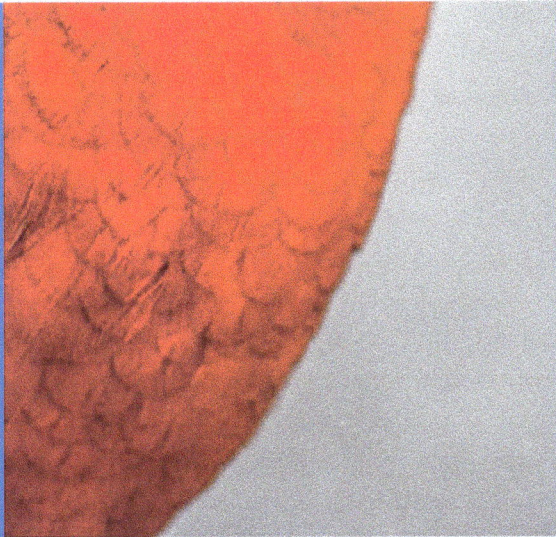

Eastern Spinebill

These are small honeyeaters. They have a very loud and shrill call. They eat the nectar from flowers of bushes, trees and plants. When these birds are adults, they have white on their neck and chest but are all brown underneath when young.

EASTERN SPINEBILL

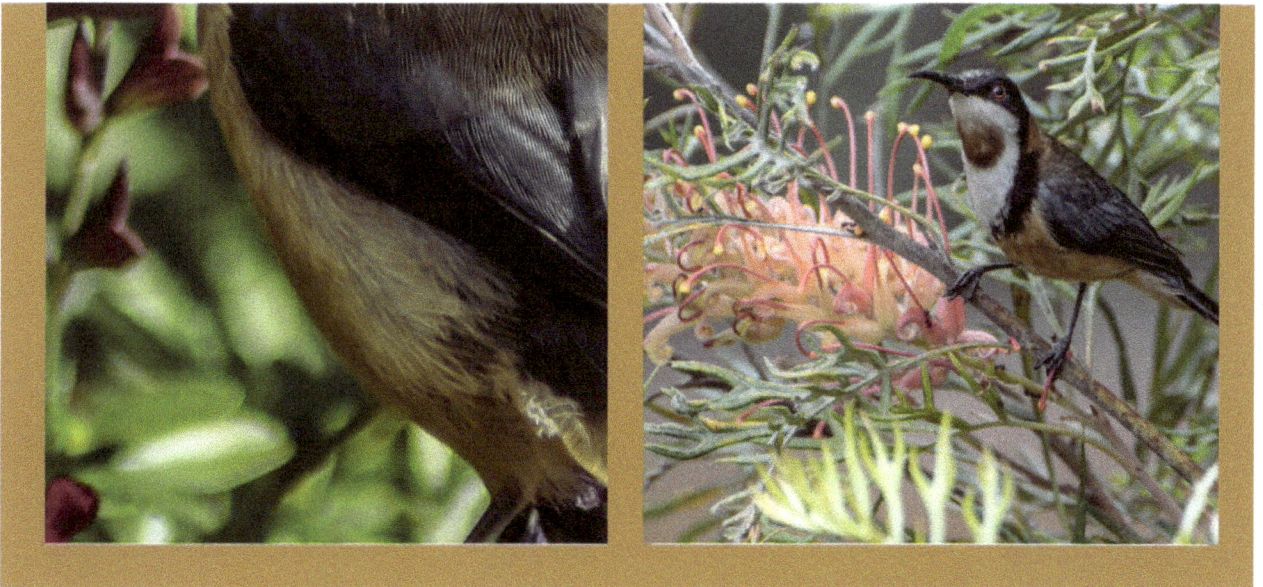

Eurasian Coot

This is a black bird, similar to the Dusky Moorhen and about the same size, but it has a white beak, red eyes and very large feet.

The Coot likes to live near or on lakes too and likes to dive into the water looking for food on the bottom of the lakes.

EURASIAN COOT

Galah or Rose-breasted Cockatoo

These are pretty birds, grey and pink with a white crest on top of their head. Sometimes called a Rose Breasted Cockatoo but usually known as a Galah. All cockatoo birds belong to the Parrot family of birds. These birds are very noisy and often hang around in flocks, screeching loudly when they take off or fly overhead.

They also like to play games, hanging upside down and being silly. Hence why sometimes people say that someone being silly is 'acting like a Galah'.

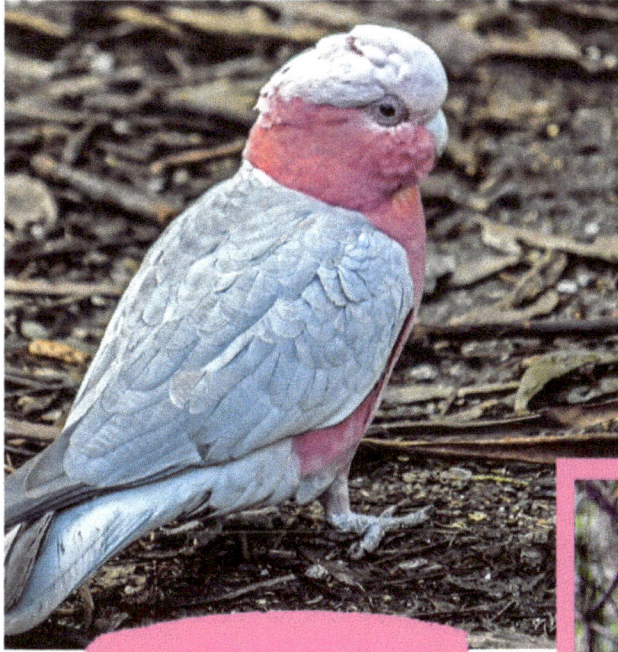

Below: These birds are showering in the rain and were swinging on the wire

GALAH

Also known as
Rose Cockatoo

Gang-gang Cockatoo

This bird has a funny name doesn't it? This cockatoo is a beautiful big bird and it is very easy to tell which is the male, and which is the female. The male has a grey body and a bright red head. The female is all grey but looks like she has a crown on her head. These birds like to eat berries and nuts from trees and make a sound like a squeaky gate.

The male on the left,
the female below

**GANG GANG
COCKATOO**

Golden Whistler

This is a small bird with a very loud whistling call. Again, the male and female birds are very different. The males have a grey back, bright yellow underneath and white throat outlined in black. The females are brown and grey. They like to hang around in forests and woods and eat spiders and other insects.

The male is bright
yellow and black, and
the female is brown

GOLDEN WHISTLER

A beautiful song bird.

Grey Butcherbird

These birds are medium sized grey birds with a black head and a hooked beak. They have a loud call in the bush and not always easily seen. They will eat small lizards, small birds, insects, fruit and seeds. Butcherbirds can sometimes be mistaken for a kookaburra from a distance but are much smaller.

Below: a juvenile (young) bird

GREY BUTCHERBIRD

A beautiful song bird.

Grey Fantail

This is a pretty little bird which has a loud whistle and is grey, with some white under its throat and tail, with a light brown chest. It is called a fantail because it can spread its tail out like a fan.

This bird very rarely stays still as it's always chasing insects to eat. When it is on the ground or on a branch it will swing from one side to another almost like it is dancing. The Grey Fantail has a distinctive whistle that you will often hear before you see the bird.

Grey Fantail

King Parrots

King Parrots are big birds and can be quite loud at times too. If they think you have food for them, they will keep calling till you come.

They like to eat seeds and nuts. The male has a red body and dark green wings but the female is a light green colour with a pale red underneath. They often hang around in family groups together. The young have a mix of green and red colouring. They mostly eat seeds and fruit from trees.

KING PARROT

Laughing Kookaburra

This is a bird everyone knows, even in other countries. Do you know the song 'Kookaburra sits in the Old Gum Tree'? There are two types of Kookaburras in Australia but this particular one is here in the eastern part of Australia. They eat frogs, lizards, snakes, fish, insects, worms, even rats and mice so are a good friend to have in your garden although they can be naughty if you have a fish pond as they might steal the fish! Anything they catch, they will beat against the branch of a tree to kill it first before eating it whole.

LAUGHING KOOKABURRA

Little Pied Cormorant

Pied means two coloured. In this case the Little Black Cormorant is black and white. They have a black back and wings and a white neck and breast. Adults have white above their eyes.

There are also Little Black Cormorants and larger Black and Pied Cormorants too. All these cormorants are found in wetland areas, lakes and the sea and are fish eaters. They dive into the water to catch their food.

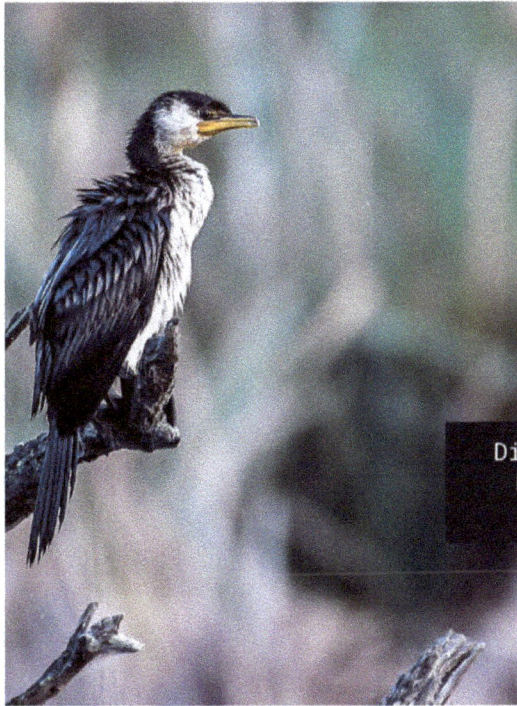

Did you know that Pied means two colours?

The Pied Cormorant will often sit on pieces of wood in lakes and waterways to watch for food

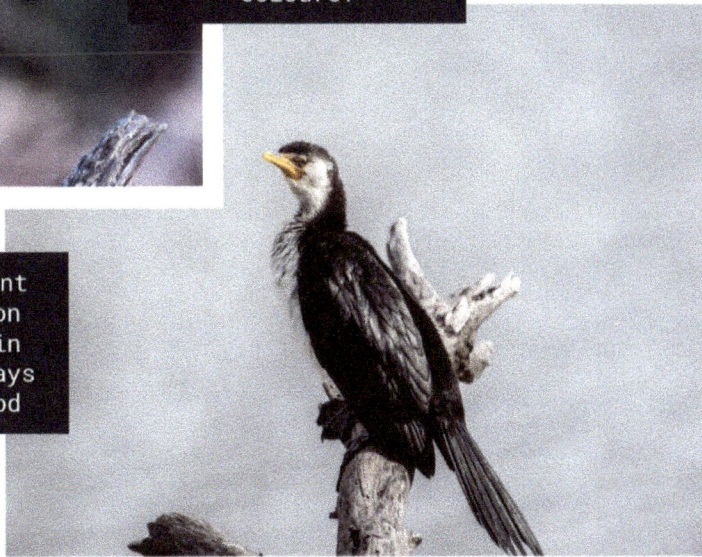

Magpie

I bet you've seen these around everywhere. A black and white bird with a beautiful song known as a warble. The adult males have a white patch on their back but the females are more grey. They usually hang around in family groups and they search the ground for insects, and they will eat food given by humans. During their breeding season, they have been known to swoop anyone walking near where their nests are.

M A G P I E

New Holland Honeyeater

This bird is mostly black and white but has yellow sides on the tail. They are medium sized and can be quite noisy. They love to eat nectar from flowers as well as fruit, insects and spiders. Often they can be seen alone, but sometimes also in groups.

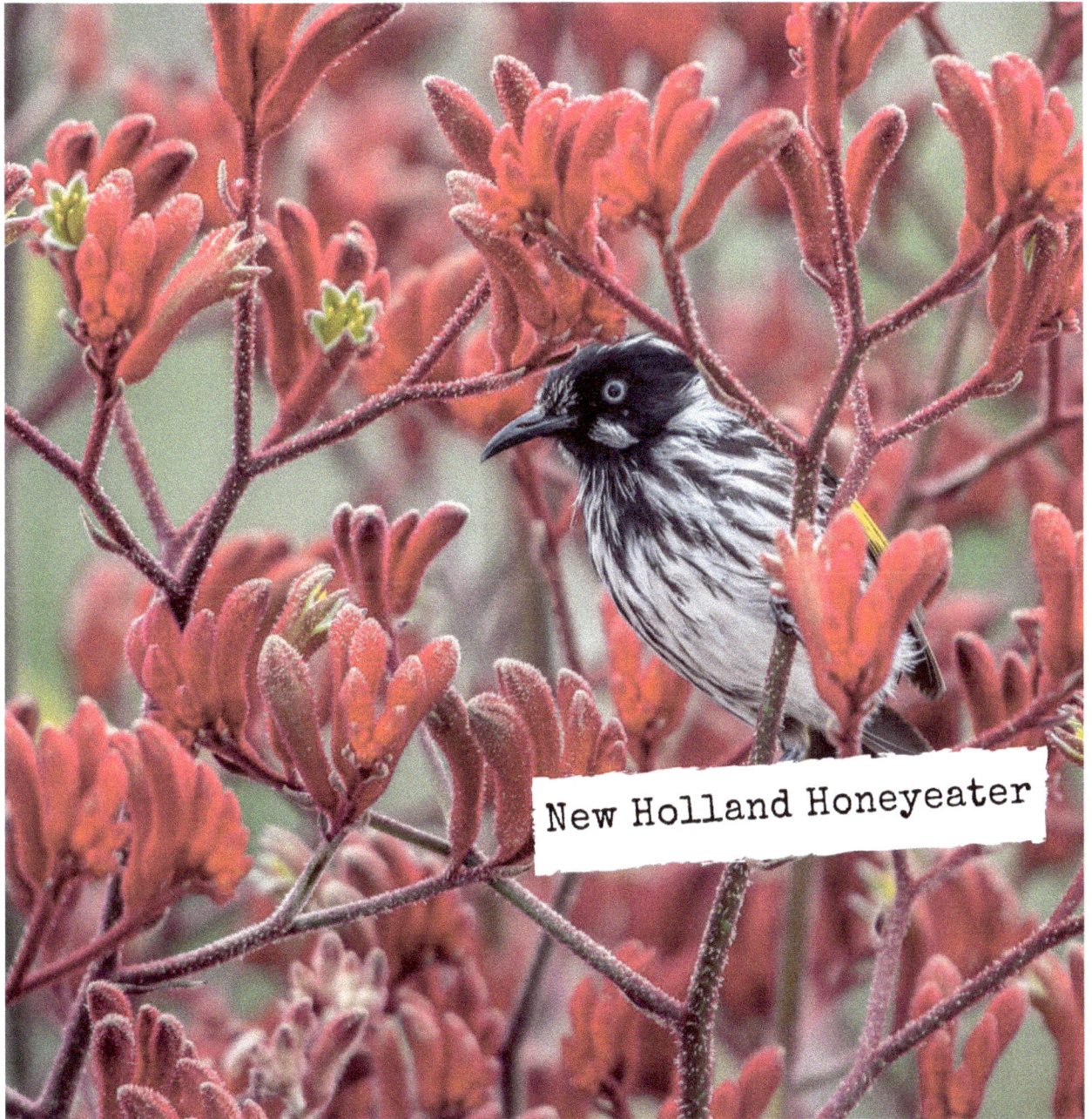

New Holland Honeyeater

Australian Pelican

Pelicans are very large birds that live near water. They can be found in lakes and by the sea and rivers. They are very graceful flying birds and can travel great distances. They feed on fish.

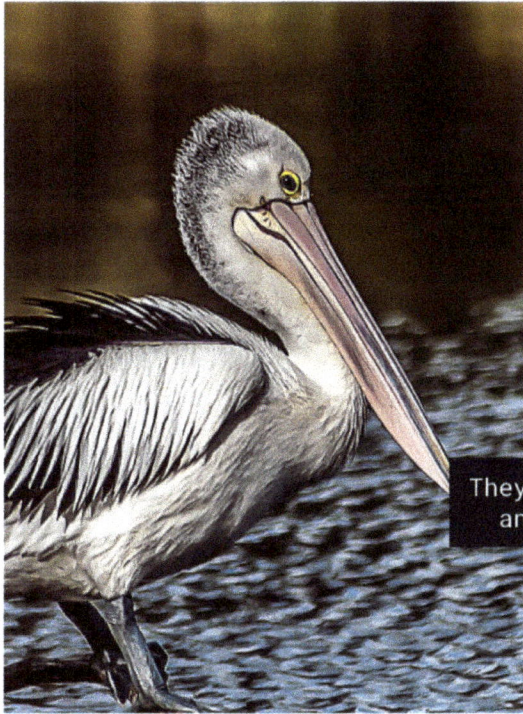

They are a large bird
and live by water

The Pelican looks
graceful in flight

Pied Currawong

This is a black bird with white tips on its wings and tail and has yellow eyes. It has a very strange call and they hang around in groups.

They are large birds and live in forests and woodlands but also hang around towns. They will eat fruit, insects, small lizards, caterpillars and berries, but are also known for going through bins for food.

PIED CURRAWONG

Purple Swamphen

Purple Swamphens live in wetland areas, lakes and rivers. They often nest amongst the plant life in these waterways. They have a purple underside, black wings and a white tip on their tails. They also have a red beak, red eyes, legs and very long red feet.

These birds eat the soft shoots of reeds and rushes as well as frogs and snails. Apparently, they will eat ducklings too, if they can catch them. They use their long toes for grasping food.

PURPLE SWAMPHEN

Rainbow Lorikeet

The Rainbow Lorikeet is called this because of all the colours it has, just like a rainbow. It is such a pretty and brightly coloured bird, but it is also a very noisy bird! They usually hang around in groups together. They like to eat flowers, fruits, seeds and some insects.

Rainbow Lorikeet

Australian Raven

Ravens are often mistakenly called Crows. They are all black with white eyes.

They eat grains, fruits, insects, small animals, and will steal chicken eggs and other eggs from nests if they can find them. They will also eat any dead animals found on the road.

Raven

They like to steal things

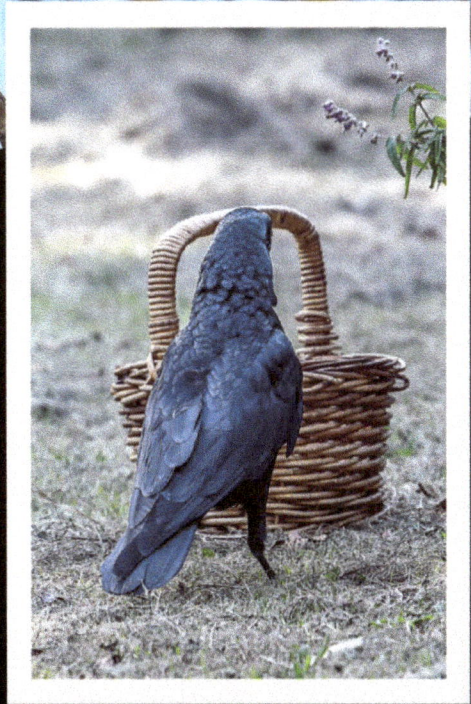

Rufous Fantail

These are very pretty little birds and are insect eaters. They have a small squeak sound and love to dart here and there to catch insects. They swing from side to side, similar to Grey Fantails, and spread out their tails too. They have a beautiful reddish brown rump and the same colour on their eyebrows.

RUFOUS FANTAIL

Satin Bowerbird

The Satin Bowerbird is an interesting bird with brilliant blue eyes. It is a medium-sized bird.

The adult male has a dark blue-black colour which looks shiny but the young birds and females are a different, lighter colour and are known as 'green' birds.

The male bird keeps mostly on its own but the 'green' birds hang around in groups. They feed mostly on fruits but also insects and, in winter, on leaves. The male adult bird likes to collect blue things to decorate its bower to attract female birds.

Both photos show a 'green' bowerbird

SATIN BOWERBIRD

Satin Flycatcher

This is a small blue-black and white bird with a small crest. The females have an orange-red chin and lighter colouring.

The Satin Flycatcher likes to stay around forests and woodlands, preferably where it is wetter. They are insect eaters.

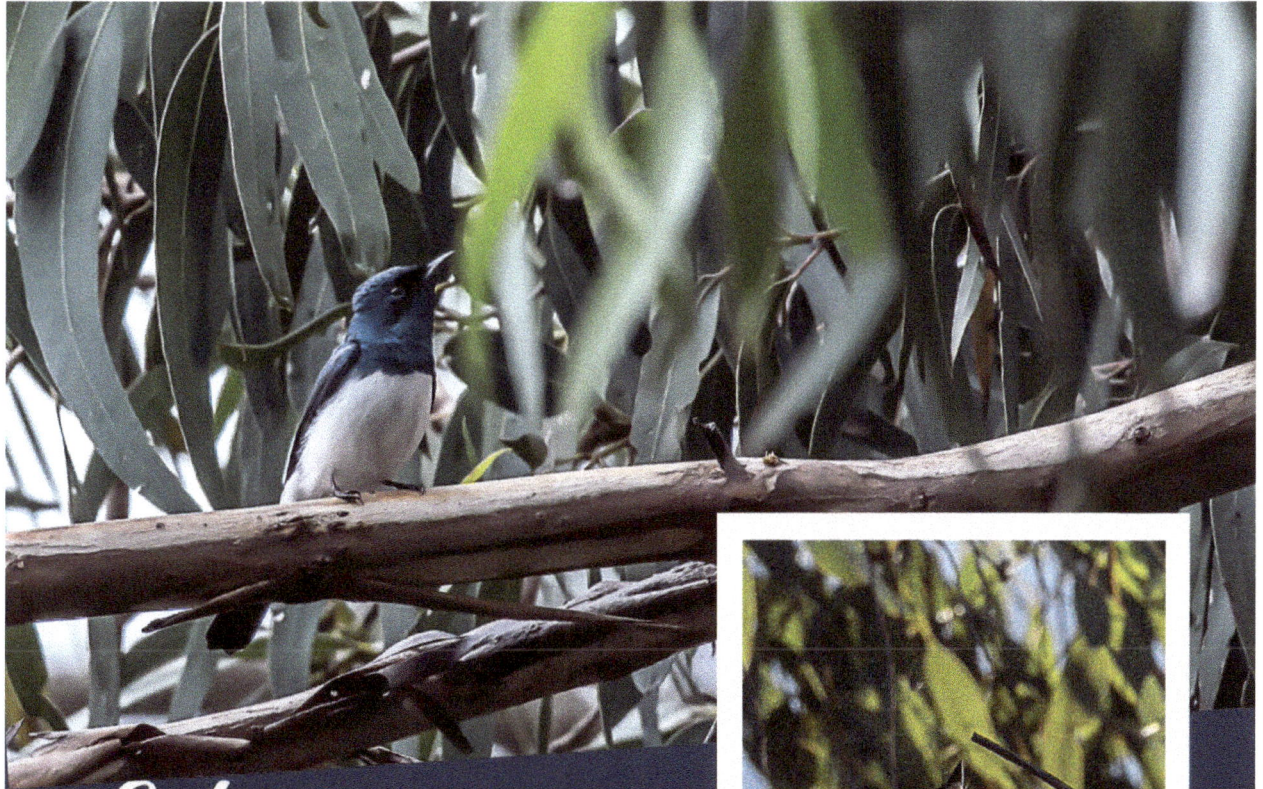

Satin
Flycatcher

Male above
Female to the right

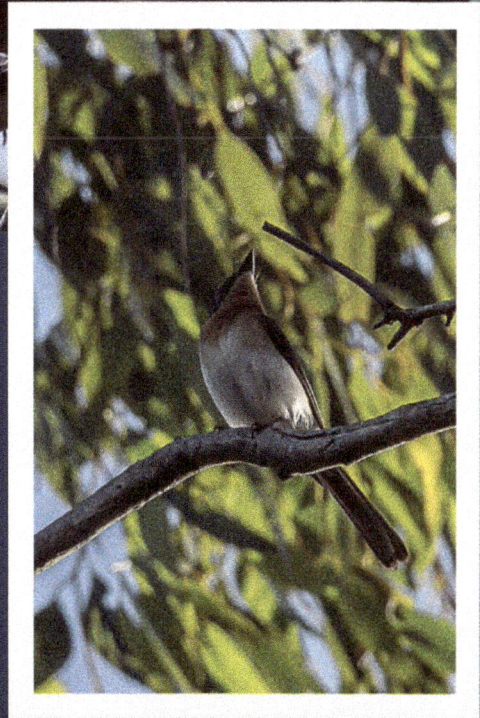

Spotted Pardalote

This is a very tiny and pretty bird which loves to hang around gum trees. The bird is covered in spots and has a beautiful yellow throat and a red rump. It eats insects and also the sugary parts that are discharged from leaves.

A very small bird

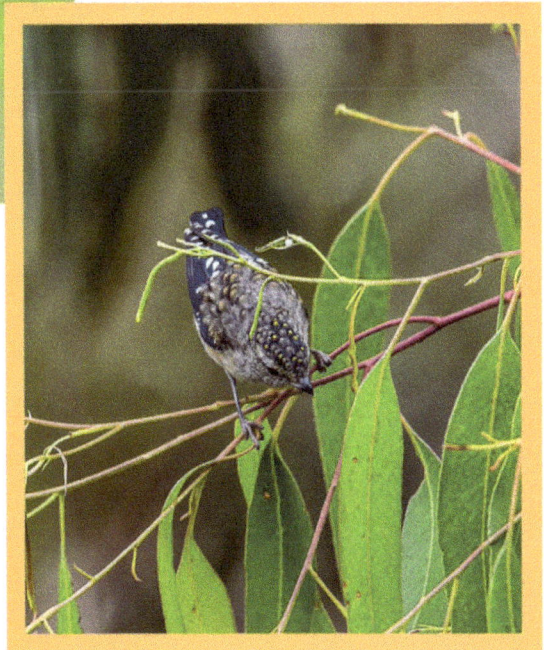

SPOTTED
PARDALOTE

Sulphur-crested Cockatoos

These are big and very loud and noisy birds, mainly white with a yellow crest. They also have yellow under their wings. They are very comical and like to hang upside down from trees and power lines in the street. Females have a red-brown eye and males have a brown eye. They like to eat berries, seeds, nuts and roots and will dig up flower bulbs. They are funny to watch.

Sulphur-
Crested
Cockatoo

Superb Fairy-wren

The Superb Fairy-wren is another bird where the male is quite different to the female. They are a tiny bird and make a high pitched squeaking sound. The males are a beautiful blue and black and the females are brown with red around their eyes. The young are speckled in colour till they grow older. These birds are also insect eaters and can often be found on the ground and in low lying bushes.

SUPERB FAIRY-WREN

Superb Lyrebird

This is an amazing bird with an ability to copy almost any sound it hears. When they are in breeding plumage the males have a beautiful long tail but the females don't. The males like to make the nest and then dance and sing to attract the females in the area. Their tails are shaped like the musical instrument called a Lyre. They live mostly on the ground but sleep in trees at night. Lyrebirds eat insects, spiders, worms and sometimes seed. They scratch the ground to look for food. Did you know that the Lyrebird is the emblem of the Dandenong Ranges?

The Lyrebird is often hard to find but easy to hear

They like to scratch on the ground for food

Tawny Frogmouths

These birds are often mistaken to be Owls but they are not Owls they are Frogmouths. They can hide in trees and make themselves look like the branches of the trees they are in. They eat nighttime insects, worms, slugs, snails, small lizards, frogs and birds. They will drop to the ground from the tree to land on their prey. They also catch moths in flight.

TAWNY FROGMOUTH

Wattle Bird

We have two types of Wattlebirds here in the Dandenong Ranges. The Little Wattlebird and the Red Wattlebird.

Both are honeyeaters and the Red Wattlebird looks similar to the Little Wattlebird except they have a red wattle on both sides of their neck.

WATTLEBIRD

White-eared Honeyeater

This is a medium-sized honeyeater and is olive-green in colour on the top and a lighter green underneath. It has a grey cap with a black face and white ear patches.

They are found mostly in forests, woodlands and shrublands. These honeyeaters feast on insects mainly but also like nectar, fruit and honeydew. They build their nests close to the ground in shrubs.

Medium-sized
honeyeater

WHITE-EARED
HONEYEATER

White-faced Herons

These are large birds that live near wetlands, lakes and rivers. They have long legs and very long beaks. They are grey with a white face and make a growling noise when annoyed. They have a slow way of flying and look amazing in the air. These birds feed on fish, insects and amphibians, like frogs.

Have you seen one of
these birds? Maybe
near a lake, or in a
paddock.

**WHITE-FACED
HERON**

White-throated Tree creeper

This is a small bird that runs up the side of trees, seeking ants to eat as well as nectar. It is dark brown with a white throat and white streaks on its underside. It has a very loud call for a tiny bird. These birds like to live in forests and woodlands.

Very good at climbing trees

WHITE-THROATED TREECREEPER

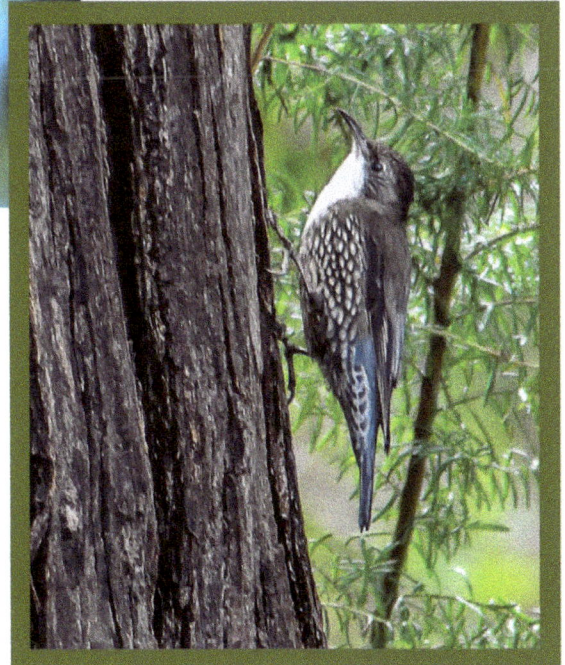

Willie Wagtail

The Willie Wagtail is also a fantail and the largest of this type of bird in Australia. It has a black back and white breast with white eyebrows – although very tiny.

They are present in many areas of Australia as well as here in the Dandenong Ranges. They like to live in open forests and woodlands and they are often found near wetlands too. These birds are insect eaters and often dart around in the air and on the ground while hunting food.

Willie Wagtail

Another fantail bird

Wood Ducks

Ducks live by lakes, rivers, dams and ponds and usually in pairs. Like some other bird species, the males are different to the females, grey in colour with two dark stripes down their backs. The females have a speckled tummy. They can be found on farmlands or properties that have a suitable water source and will raise their young there. They nest in the trees and when their ducklings are hatched and ready to leave the nest they have to jump down, one by one, to the ground and then follow their parents to the water source nearby. They eat grasses, clover, herbs and sometimes insects.

The ducks sleep and nest in trees

A family of wood ducks on the move

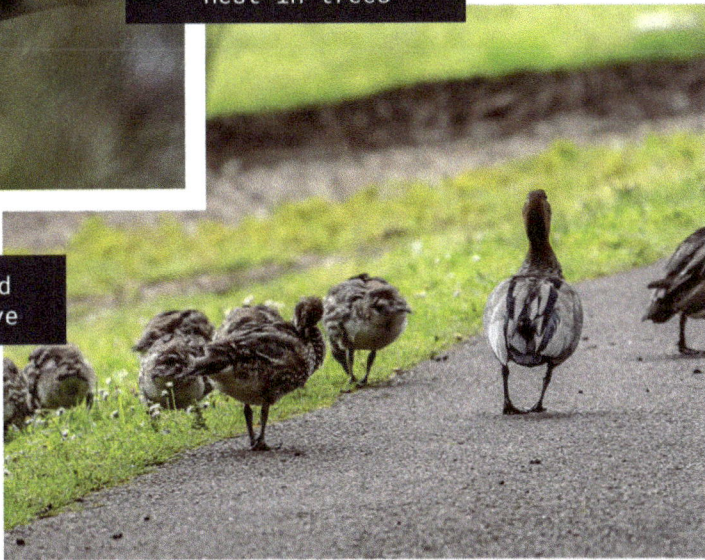

Yellow-tailed Black Cockatoo

This is a large bird from the parrot family. They are mostly black with yellow on the sides of their heads and a yellow strip under their tails. The males have a pink circle around their eyes and the females have a grey circle.

They often stay together in small groups and you can hear them making a crooning sound when in hakea trees eating on nuts. I think it's a happy sound. They also eat pinecones and seeds from ground plants.

YELLOW-TAILED BLACK COCKATOO

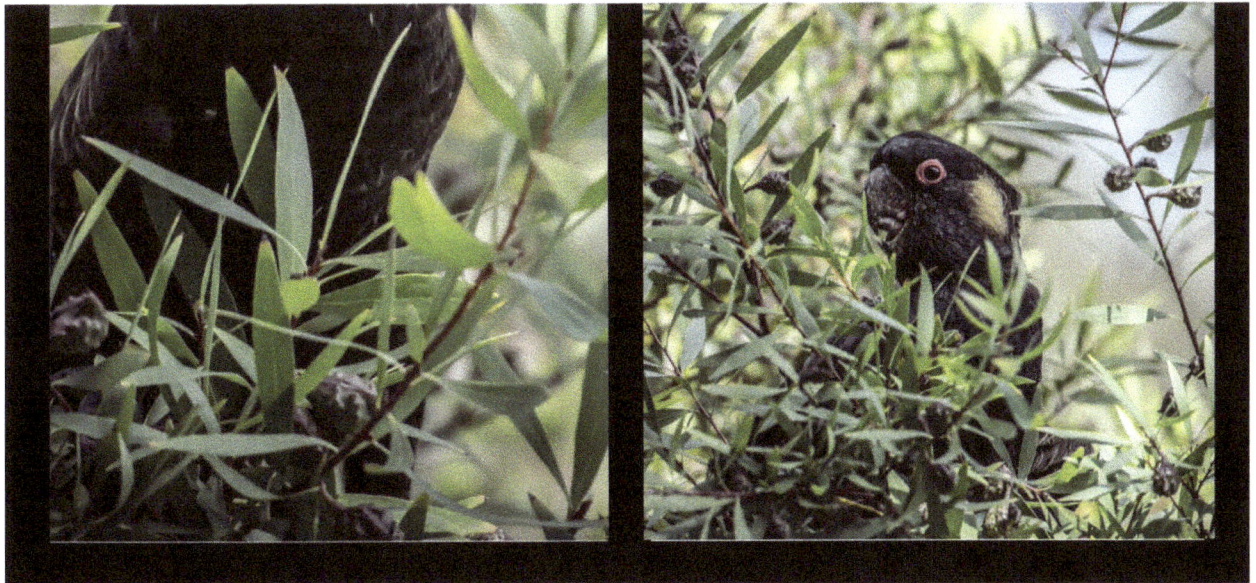

How many of these birds have you seen? Write them down on these pages when you see them so you can keep a record.

Name of Bird	Date seen	Where seen

Name of Bird	Date seen	Where seen

This is the first of a book written for children by Kathie.

If you would like to give her feedback, or contact her about anything else, you can find her via her website.

www.dandenong-ranges-photography.com.au

www.ingramcontent.com/pod-product-compliance
Lightning Source LLC
Chambersburg PA
CBHW051618030426
42334CB00030B/3236